NARROW MINDED

A 31-Day Challenge for Radical Living

DANTE MOORE

PHILADELPHIA, PENNSYLVANIA

NARROW MINDED: A 31-Day Challenge for Radical Living

Published by PTP Publishing, Philadelphia, PA.

ISBN: 978-1-7320494-1-3 Paperback
ISBN: 978-1-7320494-0-6 Hardcover
ISBN: 978-1-7320494-2-0 E-Book

Cover Design: Fatima Burke

Interior Design & Typesetting: John Ruffin | 5937 Design

First Printing 2018

Printed in the United States of America

I dedicate this book to my wife, D'ani Moore who has always been an anchor and support to remind me of what is most important. Thank you for helping me to be comfortable with developing a narrow mind. This first one is for you!

Acknowledgments

This challenge is written with everyone in mind who has willingly sought to bear the rugged cross of Jesus Christ in the midst of much cultural adversity. Keep counting the cost, knowing that when it is all added up it will be well worth the glorious treasures that await those who stood firm and pursued the narrow road that only few have found.

Thank you to my beloved wife D'ani for her support, prayers, and prompting throughout this entire journey. Thank you for encouraging me to finish what the Lord has started and standing behind me every step of the way. I love you babe!

A special thanks goes out to a fellow author and servant in the Lord, Cheryl A. Johnson for her assistance in revising my original thoughts. I also would like to thank my brother in the faith, Matthew Francis for his editorial assistance. I appreciate you both for being a part of this process.

Last but not least I thank my Lord and Savior Jesus Christ for giving me the Holy Spirit by which His power allowed me to pen the very words before you. The words hit me first and challenged me just as much as I pray they impact you. The thoughts, scriptures, questions, and prayers that were derived in this book, I have truly gleaned from myself. I know the Lord has written this not only for me and through me, but for the edification of His body. I pray it blesses you.

We are Made 4 Moore!

In a time when following the crowd seems more fitting and Christians are called to be politically correct rather than Biblical, *NARROW MINDED* stands out as writings for the revolutionary. This is no ordinary devotional, the knowledge contained in these pages, challenges the believer to stop merely being inspired and to start living against the grain. *NARROW MINDED* individuals, by nature, are often thought to be intolerant of other views, possess tunnel vision, and believe their way as the right one. However, doesn't that adequately describe the mentality of the true Jesus of the scriptures? Was not His mindset focused on a path rarely traveled, the narrow road that led to what He told us was eternal life? If taken at its value this book will challenge, encourage, offend, instruct, and strengthen the modern day Christian to live expediently to the calling of truly being not of this world.

NARROW MINDED

Reverend Sandra Reed,

May God bless and keep you in your faith walk. Stay on the Narrow Path, pursuing the father's will.

Visit Us:

www.Made4Moore.com

MADE 4 MOORE

DAY 001

"Your deliverance is not in the information, it's in the application."

DAY 001

But prove yourselves doers of the word, and not merely hearers who delude themselves

JAMES 1:22 (NASB)

I remember when I was in high school, so anxious to move to the next phase in my life and get my driver's license. I studied my driver's manual day and night until I knew every sign, law, signal, and method. When I took my permit test I had to show evidence of what I learned. Like a good student, I keyed in the answers I had memorized and studied just moments before. Despite passing the test, I still couldn't drive on the road alone because all I had done so far was show that I had the knowledge that would permit me the privilege to apply it. It's not enough to know; you must apply. When it was time for my driver's test I had to apply my knowledge without books, signs, multiple choice answers, or easy ways out. The only way I would be able to go to the next level and receive my license was by demonstrating what I knew to be true about the laws of the road. Such is life. You won't be delivered into the next phase of your life by just reviewing raw information. Data is merely facts and statistics collected together for reference or analysis. You can take in a tremendous amount of data every day, but it will have no effect on your outcomes without intentional application. What do you need to be delivered from today? You've heard enough words providing you with KNOWLEDGE, now it's time to APPLY IT!

DAY 001

1. What areas of your life do you find most difficult to apply God's Word to?___________

___

___

___

___

___

___

___

___

___

2. Name the fears that you face when it comes to applying what you know in those areas. ___

___

___

___

___

___

___

___

___

___

DAY 001

////// **CHALLENGE:** Today, select just one area of your life and apply God's Word to it.

Write down your results. ____

____

____

____

____

____

____

____

____

____

LORD,

I pray that today I would live a life that is not filled with robust knowledge of you and no common application. Guide me as I attempt to walk by the Spirit and trust in your word. While intellect is good, it does not serve as a substitute for intimacy. Strengthen me by Your power to apply what I know today, in Jesus' Name.

AMEN.

DAY 002

"The best thing a Christian can ever say is: I can't fix it."

DAY 002

For by grace you have been saved through faith. And this is not your own doing; it is the gift of God, not a result of works, so that no one may boast.

EPHESIANS 2:8-9 (ESV)

There is an overwhelming desire to feel like we have to fix everything that is seemingly wrong, in order to make things right. We are so used to doing everything on our own, and in our own strength that we approach our relationship with God the same way. I'm quite certain you have said at one point or another that you are "trying to get your relationship right with the Lord," creating a checklist of what you need to fix so that God can use you, or see you as righteous. Newsflash! God sees you as righteous because He sees Christ as righteous, and you are in Christ! Our faulty attempt to try to fix our condition simply makes the justification plea that was given on our behalf seem less than adequate. It has already been said that at times we will miss the mark (sin). That's why the only thing God can and will respond to is full faith in Him alone. God doesn't commend you for trying alone; He only condemns you for trying alone. Stop trying...start relying!

1. What areas in your life have you not given to God because you believe you can fix them under your own power? ____

____

____

____

____

____

____

____

____

____

2. Faith and Fear. Use one of these two words to describe why you haven't given that area completely to God. ____

____

____

____

____

____

____

____

____

____

DAY 002

////// **CHALLENGE:** Admit that you are broken beyond human repair and that only God Himself can put you back together. Pray for full faith to let go of your life and trust God completely. ____

____

____

____

____

____

____

____

____

____

LORD,

it's so difficult for me to give everything to you because I haven't been that open with anyone before. Help me, by the strength of your might, to surrender all to you so that you can fix me. Continue to sanctify me and make me comfortable in resting in you, knowing that you who have begun a good work in me will complete it. I release my life completely into your hands, in Jesus' Name,

AMEN.

DAY 003

“The truth won’t change because you got offended. Get used to it.”

DAY 003

The sum of your word is truth, and every one of your righteous rules endures forever.

PSALMS 119:160 (ESV)

Truth is an absolute and is unwavering. Often times when the words of truth are spoken, we are offended because we are living in an area of falsehood and denial. In our culture today many want to live in their individual truth and not by the ultimate truth. Therefore the truth always sounds like hate to those who hate the truth. By its very nature, the truth is indivisible and will not change. This leaves one thing that must change – YOU. The truth will never conform to fit our subjective opinions, mixed ideologies, or alternative patterns of life. It will remain as consistent and objective as the statement: "And just as it is appointed for man to die once, and after that comes judgment." – Hebrews 9:27 (ESV) The sum of God's word is Truth, and Christ, in His bodily form, stated He was that Truth. If the truth can be equated to God Himself, we know for sure then that it is immutable – which means unchanging. With truth comes a standard by which you can examine your life today and see if there are any areas of falsehood that have to be confronted. It is better to walk and live in the truth than to operate in a lie. For a while you may be fully convinced, but nevertheless, you are still deceived.

DAY 003

1. By holding God's Word up as the standard of truth, what areas of falsehood do you see commonly displayed around you (in your culture/community)? ____________________

2. If you were to uphold God's Word as the standard of truth for your life as well, what areas of falsehood could you see, presently, within you? ____________________

////// **CHALLENGE:** For every area of falsehood you pulled out in yourself (not in others), write down a statement of God's truth. Every morning remind yourself that God's truth is not going to change and the lie you once believed has to. Do this by speaking God's truth out loud each day until you begin to believe it over the unraveling lies.________________

____

____

____

____

____

____

____

____

FATHER,

I pray my eyes would be opened to the many areas that I have been deceived and manipulated. There are so many schemes and tactics that seek to divert me from the path of following you, but I will hold fast onto your word. Many times the Word of God offends my own thoughts or opinions, but help me to know that your truth is for my good. I want to solely depend on you. Illuminate my eyes that I may see clearly, in Jesus' Name.

AMEN.

DAY 004

//////////////

"Life is a maybe. Death is for sure. Sin is the cause. Christ is the cure."

//////////////

DAY 004

Jesus said to her, "I am the resurrection and the life.
Whoever believes in me, though he die, yet shall he live.

JOHN 11:25 (ESV)

We are truly in the day of the walking dead, and before Christ came into our lives, we were also dead men walking. Our world has been hit hard by a generational plague and we are sin sick. Every day we see walking corpses that have all the vital signs and motor functions of healthy human beings. Therefore, today, let's be reminded that because sin has entered into the world there is only one thing that is for sure – death. Everyone that is living does not have true life unless they have put their trust and hope in Jesus Christ alone. As cliché as this may sound, you have to be spiritually aware each day to offer the remedy and cure to our sin sick world. Introduce the sick to the Great Physician so that they may have life! For nothing is more tragic than to have a foretaste of life, only to experience it in part and apart from Christ. Jesus tells us that He is the resurrection, and with that promise we can be sure that though we die once, we will live forever when He returns!

1. If you lived today like it was your last on earth, what would you do differently?

2. Assuming that you have "the hope" and others do not, if today could be their last day on earth, how would you act differently towards them?

////// **CHALLENGE:** Whatever your answer was in question #2, apply it to at least two people that you encounter today that do not have the hope of the Lord Jesus Christ. Record your results here. ____

____

____

____

____

____

____

____

____

____

LORD,

you have saved me from the sin of this world and taken me out of the kingdom of darkness and into that of your dear Son. Thank you for redeeming me and granting me eternal life. In an effort to show my appreciation, I ask that you soften my heart to be compassionate enough to share that same message and wonderful hope with those around me. I admit I don't know everything and at times I may even be fearful, but empower me by your Holy Spirit today to share the cure of the cross of Christ for our sin! In Jesus' Name,

AMEN.

DAY 005

“You can’t be so focused putting others down, that you don’t properly lift up the Christ.”

DAY 005

Whoever slanders their neighbor in secret, I will put to silence;
whoever has haughty eyes and a proud heart, I will not tolerate.

PSALM 101:5 (NIV)

In the wake of controversial criminal court cases and racial prejudice, our nation can become divided to the point that believers begin to vehemently express their views and opinions of those standing trial. Unbeknownst to them, idle words spoken out of seemingly justifiable anger may actually be words of slander and they are in turn, committing a crime along with the accused – murder. Although to a different degree, slander is the murder of another person's character. Challenge yourself to avoid slander of another person's reputation simply because you may not understand or agree with the differences they possess. Stay focused on Christ, the One in which you serve and ask God to make you comfortable with the sanctifying process He is working in others (if they are members of the Body.) If they are not in the Body of Christ, He may use you to bring them to the revelation of Jesus Christ who will lead them to salvation and biblical repentance. Don't despise or be presumptuous of their journey. We don't always see the bigger picture, or the end goal He has in mind for the lives of others. While it is difficult to be patient and pray for those who are uniquely different from you or oppose your standard set of views, it is not impossible.

DAY 005

1. If you disagree with a person quite strongly on an issue, how do you normally handle it?

2. Would you ever discuss that person in conversation with other people and/or put them down because of their views on that issue? Why or Why not?

DAY 005

////// **CHALLENGE:** The next time you get into a disagreement or you don't understand a person's position, don't tell others first, but consult the Lord. Open up in prayer not about them but for them and for your lack of understanding. Ask God to show and give you clarity and peace about the situation. After you have finished earnestly praying, see if there is still the desire to gossip, slander, or tear that person down by your words. Prayer has the power to remove the initial carnal reactions and revert us back to giving God the glory in every situation.

____

____

____

____

____

____

FATHER GOD,

you know my heart in this matter and that I am striving to live more and more like you each day. Help me in my understanding of this particular situation that I may think like you. Allow me to die to self and crucify the sinful passions of my flesh, which would lead me to slander and gossip about another individual. Those works of the flesh do not bring you glory. Lord, I trust you to give me clarity and peace concerning this situation and I leave it in your hands.

In Jesus' Name,

AMEN.

DAY 006

"Love will stretch you, lust will break you."

DAY 006

Love is patient, love is kind. It does not envy, it does not boast, it is not proud. It is not rude, it is not self-seeking, it is not easily angered, it keeps no record of wrongs. Love does not delight in evil but rejoices with the truth. It always protects, always trusts, always hopes, always perseveres. Love never fails...

1 CORINTHIANS 13:4-8A (NIV)

Our Lord, Jesus Christ, is the embodiment of Love. Love will stretch you past your natural parameters because there is a hidden commitment that lies deep within your core and surpasses your feelings. In response to this commitment, love passionately and relentlessly pursues. The flexibility to maneuver love is supernatural and cannot come from those things that you merely lust after. Love possesses a reconciliation component that seeks to be at peace with all men and remain there by righting the wrongs that were committed, through restitution. Lust on the other hand says it loves the other person, but really means, "I love me and I'm willing to use another to show myself how much I love myself so that my desires will be fulfilled." Don't be deceived. Lust has neither conscience nor regard for consequences, and it lacks all compassion and morality. It comes from the same wicked and uncontrollable carnal nature that caused us to be cast out of the Garden of Eden. Yet, it is the nature of lust from which Christ set us free. You may be in a place where you think you are experiencing real love, but I challenge you to examine your fruits according to the scriptures, and await the end result. Lust will leave you broken, but love will make you whole.

DAY 006

1. What are some of the things you have identified in your life that you have been prone to lust after? ____________________

2. How has the pursuit of those things compromised your character as a follower of Christ, in your efforts to obtain it? ____________________

////// **CHALLENGE:** Examine your relationships, your choices for career and business exploits, and your passions and desires. Is there a simple worldly lust after these things that will result in brokenness, or a genuine and purposeful love that will produce fruit, which brings glory to God? Write them down below.________________________________

____

____

____

____

____

____

____

____

DEAR GOD,

in this life I must admit that it has been hard to forsake my lust and pursue righteousness at all times. I have been a victim to the lust of the flesh and the lust of the eyes all too often. Help me to identify with the love that is found in you through your son Jesus Christ, and to exemplify that same love to others. I pray that my pursuits and exploits would come from a place of love and purity, so that I would ultimately bring you glory and bear fruit that others may take part in. In Jesus' Name,

AMEN.

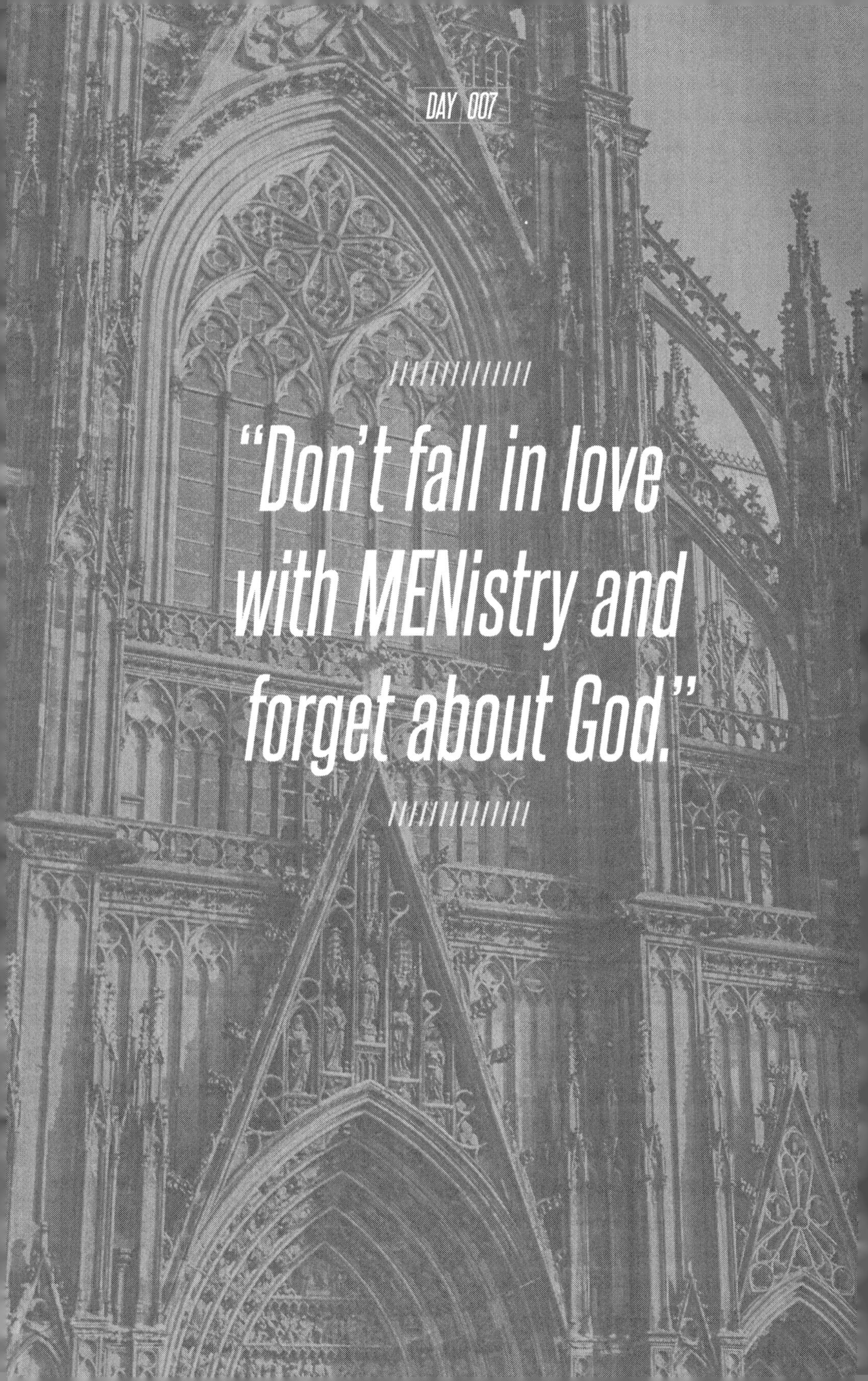
DAY 007
"Don't fall in love
with MENistry and
forget about God."

DAY 007

For am I now seeking the approval of man, or of God? Or am I trying to please man? If I were still trying to please man, I would not be a servant of Christ.

GALATIANS 1:10 (ESV)

Traveling on this journey as a disciple, you may have gotten your devotion to the Lord confused with your obligations to His people. Perhaps you've been saved for some time and now things have become routine with your Christianity. You participate in ministry more because of your position and what others think, rather than for God Himself. I remember hearing from one Pastor that I should be "acutely aware on how to separate my devotion from my duties." Be very careful today that you are not doing ministry unto MEN instead of unto GOD. While it is important that we serve one another, the main motivation should be to serve God in all that we do so He would receive all the glory. To be blinded by praise and accolades from mere men, takes your focus off your audience of One – God the Father. Jesus gave us a perfect example. Take some time to pray. More Time. Shift your focus today so that your audience of One may be well pleased.

1. How does it make you feel when you are serving others and your efforts go unrecognized? ____

____
____
____
____
____
____
____
____
____

2. What do you do with those feelings when they result in frustration, irritation, depression, or anger? ____

____
____
____
____
____
____
____
____
____

DAY 007

////// **CHALLENGE:** In a drawing exercise I want you to do the following: Isolate the position of service or ministry that causes any of the feelings described above and remove all those people who don't notice you. Next, write down God as the only authority and then your position directly under Him. Lastly, jot down what you think God expects of you in this area of service according to His Word and character. Once you have your thoughts down, challenge yourself to keep Him as the authority to serve directly under and to seek approval from.

____

____

____

____

____

____

____

DEAR GOD,

I have been under the pressure of trying to fight my feelings to please others in the area(s) I have committed to you. I am feeling over burdened and sometimes frustrated with the failure to measure up to man made standards. Please show me what it is you expect of me and restore to me the joy of serving unto you and not for man's approval. Help me to keep my focus on you alone, and to seek the words "Well Done" from your throne at the end of my days. In Jesus' Name,

AMEN.

DAY 008

//////////////

“Sin thinks it has entitlement over you since it owned you before you knew Christ. Surprise it today and remind it that it lost all rights at the cross.”

//////////////

DAY 008

Thank God! Once you were slaves of sin, but now you have obeyed with all your heart the new teaching God has given you. Now you are free from sin, your old master, and you have become slaves to your new master, righteousness.

ROMANS 6:17-18 (NLT)

Stand up, look straight into the mirror and remind yourself who you are in Christ! Sin has a way of convincing God's people that it still has dominion over your physical body and thought process. Redemption proclaims that you were bought back at a high price; that is, at the expense of your new Master who sacrificed Himself to purchase you. Sin used to live quite comfortably in your house and believes it is still welcome, but when it knocks you don't have to answer the door. Since the Holy Spirit has taken up residence within you, there is no longer a vacancy in your house! So don't feel stuck in your sin, for you now have a choice where there was once none at all. Say it aloud – "Today I choose to pick up my cross and follow Him! Today I refuse to sin."

DAY 008

1. Write down the sin by name that you deal with most frequently. Secondly, outline how it shows up in your life or what triggers cause it. ___________________________________

____

____

____

____

____

____

____

____

____

2. Describe how you feel when you've been victimized yet again by the "home invasion" of that particular sin? ____

____

____

____

____

____

____

____

____

____

DAY 008

////// **CHALLENGE:** It's time to get some home security! Write down five scriptures to say aloud and protect yourself against another home invasion. Show this sin that you are not a victim but a victor. Jot down the verses below and declare them freely in your time of temptation, then seize the way of escape! ____________________

____

____

____

____

____

____

____

____

____

GOD,

I have been dealing with the same sin for a very long time now and I'm coming to you in faith to finally be a victor instead of a victim. Lord, help me by the power of the Holy Spirit inside of me to speak your Word against sin trying to enslave me again and make me obedient to its commands. I have a new Master in Christ alone, and that is whom I serve.

In Jesus' Name,

AMEN.

DAY 009

"Don't spend your life doubting your beliefs, otherwise you may begin to believe your doubts."

DAY 009

"And immediately the father of the child cried out,
and said with tears, Lord, I believe; help my unbelief."

MARK 9:24 (KJV)

Your belief is powerful beyond measure, but FAITH is the true essence of the life of those in the Kingdom. When you place belief in yourself and your abilities to launch to greater heights, it is possible your actions could accompany that belief. Yet and still, despite your intentions and best efforts those actions may still result in failure, because your strength is limited. Now let's take a step in another direction; when you place that same belief in the God of the universe, and trust that He will launch you to the places He has promised you, the actions that accompany that belief will breed FAITH. When walking in faith, doubt is certain to invade through the fear of the unknown, but hold fast to what you first believed. While doubt is a necessary aspect of finding authentic truth, spending too much time on your doubts may result in you beginning to believe a lie. When your doubt begins to speak louder than your initial proclamation of faith, cast it out! No time for dwelling on doubt!

DAY 009

1. Be honest with yourself and write down three things that you want to believe God for, even if an inkling of doubt still remains within you. ________________________________

____

____

____

____

____

____

____

____

____

2. Take a moment and search out the following FIVE scriptures then write them down below. (James 1:6, Mark 11:24, 1 John 5:14, Proverbs 3:5, Matthew 21:21) ________________

____

____

____

____

____

____

____

____

____

////// **CHALLENGE:** After reading the Bible and placing your faith in it as God's infallible word, apply those scriptures to the three areas of your doubt. Do you still doubt? If so, keep doing it throughout the day and record your experience below. ______________________

____

____

____

____

____

____

____

____

____

LORD,

I am coming to you humbly and truly seeking to find answers to what I've been wrestling with in my heart. I believe that your Word is truth, yet I still find doubt in some areas of my life. I want to trust you completely with everything. Help me to surrender to your will the things I don't understand and cannot control, by faith alone. I believe, but help my unbelief, in Jesus' Name,

AMEN.

DAY 010

"Your pride kills every opportunity that your faith creates."

DAY 010

Pride goeth before destruction, and a haughty spirit before a fall.

PROVERBS 16:18 (KJV)

As quick as faith is birthed, it can be killed by your pride. Pride is so malicious in that it causes us to ask God for something, and then refuse to bless others or honor God with it. Imagine you have believed God for some great things and they have finally begun to manifest themselves. You were faithful and committed to trusting in the Lord's perfect timing and He was equally as faithful to bless you in return. Subtly, pride snuck in the back door and has sabotaged everything you believed God for, because once you've received it you forgot to honor Him with it. Instead, you opt to gloat about all you have done and sometimes even complain that you're not further, as if you deserved more. If you sought God for it and He brought it to you, you can't kick Him out of it, and expect it to last. Do not be mistaken, pride is at the root of all sin and should you choose to give it any breathing room, it will suffocate your blessing and push you further back than your initial starting point. Keep an eye out for pride and eliminate it on sight.

1. Identify three major areas in your life that you continually struggle with as a Christian.

____

____

____

____

____

____

____

____

____

2. Trace back and document how pride is systemically the root of these three issues.____

____

____

____

____

____

____

____

____

____

DAY 010

////// **CHALLENGE:** Cleaning up the collateral damage! Pride comes before the fall, and most often we don't fall alone in an open area but on top of others bruising them on our way down. If you are serious about removing pride to let your faith soar, take those three major areas in your life and highlight who was/is part of the collateral damage. Once identified, seek forgiveness for how things were handled and rectify any wrongs.______

____

____

____

____

____

____

____

____

GOD,

I know I have trusted you with many things and yet I still struggle with others. Help me to identify the source of my struggle, which is rooted in pride and reverse it by putting total faith in you. In Jesus' Name,

AMEN.

DAY 011

"Christians are not celebrities, we are the underdogs"

DAY 011

But if some of the branches were broken off, and you, although a wild olive shoot, were grafted in among the others and now share in the nourishing root of the olive tree, do not be arrogant toward the branches. If you are, remember it is not you who support the root, but the root that supports you. Then you will say, "Branches were broken off so that I might be grafted in." That is true. They were broken off because of their unbelief, but you stand fast through faith. So do not become proud, but fear. For if God did not spare the natural branches, neither will he spare you.

ROMANS 11:17-21 (ESV)

The temptation to want to be praised and celebrated, in some fashion, arises in every human being. It may seem fitting for a person who has committed their life to the Lord Jesus Christ to be recognized and celebrated for that decision. That's where it starts. Then, rationalizing the celebration of your many merits for the Body of Christ will come into the equation. Pretty soon you will want others to extol your spiritual gifts, your position, your previous works, and practically your mere existence! Before you get ahead of yourself today, remember this very fact – You are an underdog. Most, if not all of us were not even in the original plan of redemption designed for Holy Israel, God's chosen people as far as we knew. We were merely grafted into the plan of salvation by the Blood of the Lord Jesus Christ. We were selected for adoption because of His suffering and rejection. So even with our current positions and "social religious status", we're nothing but a bunch of twerps in skirts and goofs in suits. Stay low; remain an underdog.

1. What do you personally believe makes you different as a Christian from others who have accepted Jesus Christ? ____

____

____

____

____

____

____

____

____

____

2. How has your understanding of who you are in Christ changed the way you view and treat others? ____

____

____

____

____

____

____

____

____

____

DAY 011

////// **CHALLENGE:** Imagine for a moment that you adopted a child and they ignored your biological children, mistreated/taunted their other adopted siblings, and saw him or herself as superior because they were adopted. What would be your first reaction to that child? How would you deal with that child? How do you suppose God would deal with a situation like this?

____

____

____

____

____

____

____

____

____

FATHER,

help us today to not get ahead of ourselves. Let our only boast be in Christ the Lord. We understand that it was only by your sovereign grace that you adopted us. Let us remain low and humble as we continue on our journey.

In Jesus' Name,

AMEN.

DAY 012

"Many say they would die for Christ, but we can't even live for Him."

DAY 012

I have been crucified with Christ. It is no longer I who live, but Christ who lives in me. And the life I now live in the flesh I live by faith in the Son of God, who loved me and gave himself for me.

GALATIANS 2:20 (ESV)

Your life in Christ involves "dying-to-self" daily. Let's assume you feel like a martyr for the cause today, and boldly proclaim 'I will die for Christ.' Have you committed to that death of the flesh on a consistent basis first? If the carnal thoughts and secular values that consistently infiltrate your mind aren't being killed with the Word of God, can you be sure you're ready to physically die for what you say you believe in? It's much harder to sacrifice your entire being than it is to renew your mind with the Word of God and walk in the Spirit. Think about this for a moment, Jesus who is God in the flesh, had second thoughts about dying on the cross while in the garden of Gethsemane. Don't be so quick to say what you would do. That choice was a difficult one even for Christ and he foreknew He was sent here on the narrow road to die. Focus on living this life unto Him by denying yourself daily by the power of the Holy Spirit.

DAY 012

1. Do you find it difficult to change your mind daily to the pattern of Christ-like submission? Why or why not? ____

____

____

____

____

____

____

____

____

____

2. How does your view of death shape how you presently live? ____________________

____

____

____

____

____

____

____

____

____

////// **CHALLENGE:** Examine your heart: Are you abandoning your current responsibility to live for Christ today as His representative on earth, with the hope to escape by death?

____

____

____

____

____

____

____

____

____

LORD,

today I pray that you would give me a big picture focus of your Kingdom and who you are. Renew in me the desire to be your disciple and ambassador here on earth until your glorious return at the second coming. In Jesus' Name,

AMEN.

DAY 013

"Sick of treating God like a whore? The one night stands end today!"

DO NOT DISTURB

DAY 013

Do not love the world or anything in the world.
If anyone loves the world, love for the Father is not in them.

1 JOHN 2:15 (NIV)

You had a euphoric time in God's presence and the intimacy level was sky high. You truly felt Him doing great things within you and during that time you worshiped Him unabashed. Unashamed, you made vows and promises and decreed you would NEVER do "it" again. You felt like your fellowship with the Creator of the universe was in full harmony and your purpose was re-established. Satisfaction saturated your soul. Good vibes all around. Then you paid Him, asked "same time again next week?" and left. The next couple days, weeks, months were business as usual. No intimacy, no connection, no satisfaction. God gave you your "fix" and you kicked Him to the curb until you were feeling low again. In order to have full satisfaction in the Lord alone, this relationship has to be permanent. You have engaged in one-night stands long enough, it's time you settle down and marry the Bride-Groom.

DAY 013

1. What typically happens after you experience God's presence in a way that leaves you feeling complete and restored?____

2. List 5 adjectives that you would use to describe God in your most fulfilling moments.

DAY 013

////// **CHALLENGE:** When you engage God on a daily basis with all of your heart, He is glorified in that He sees Himself at work in you. The adjectives you listed in question #2 are mirrored in you to God as He sees Himself in you through your worship. Glorify God today by making this relationship one of reciprocity through reading the word, worship, and prayer. ______

____

____

____

____

____

____

____

____

____

LORD,

I desire to be more like you and have a full time relationship with you. My worship makes me more like you and brings you glory. Remind me to set aside my own selfish desires that I might find full satisfaction in you. In Jesus' Name,

AMEN.

DAY 014

"Charisma is not the anointing."

DAY 014

Having a form of godliness, but denying the power thereof: from such turn away.

2 TIMOTHY 3:5 (KJV)

The calling that God has placed on the life of an individual cannot be limited to one form of expression. Do not be carried away by charisma. While they may seem endearing and alluring, one's personality traits and gifts should not be confused with God's divine anointing. There is a very real anointing that the Lord has placed on those whom He has called His own. It is the anointing that makes one stand out from the rest. The anointing that comes from God ought to be displayed in the characteristics that we have come to know as the fruit of the Spirit. They are love, joy, peace, forbearance, kindness, goodness, faithfulness, gentleness, and self-control (Galatians 5:22-23). Don't compare yourself to others, who some see as super Christians (but really are not). Think instead of Jesus. People perceived Him to be one way but did not know who He really was. His anointing showed Him as a LAMB but He had the power of a LION! The same anointing caused wise men and shepherds alike to come and worship Him at His birth. He had yet to perform one miracle or say one word. Let others think about you what they will, but let the power of God's anointing show them who you truly are.

DAY 014

1. Has there ever been a time where you relied on your own strength instead of God's power to do something? How did it turn out? ______________________________

2. Do you feel God has anointed (divinely elected and chosen) you for a purpose? If so, what is it for while here on earth?______________________________

////// **CHALLENGE:** Study Ephesians 4:11-13 and seek God for understanding of the scriptures. ____

____

____

____

____

____

____

____

____

____

GOD,

in a time where deception and false prophets run rampant guard my mind from being led astray. I pray that you would reveal in me your divine purpose for my life as well as the calling that has been placed on me. As I gain more understanding provide me with an anointing that will make room for me to operate freely with those gifts. In Jesus' Name,

AMEN.

DAY 015

“Sin is a big deal, but God has a bigger will.”

DAY 015

Therefore, there is now no condemnation for those who are in Christ Jesus, because through Christ Jesus the law of the Spirit who gives life has set you free from the law of sin and death.

ROMANS 8:1-2 (NIV)

You can't afford to take sin lightly; however you can't over dramatize it either. Your enemy, Satan, has a very conniving way to keep you in a guilt-ridden state, believing God's divine grace cannot extend to all areas of sin in your life. The Father of Lies is back at it. The sin of the world was taken and dealt with and defeated on the cross at Calvary. During that time God included a provision in His will for your life. It sounds like this: "Where sin abounded, grace did much more abound."– Romans 5:20 (KJV) Today, as a believer, you don't have to be subject to living a lifestyle of unrepentant, habitual, and unacknowledged sin. Christ conquered sin on the cross, therefore in your acceptance of Him, sin has no more authority over you. Now you have a choice to never sin again! You have the Holy Spirit, which will keep you walking in the path of righteousness. However, if you do sin, don't beat yourself up about it because there is more good news! Forgiveness is available. Confess to God, repent and make restitution where necessary and walk in the Spirit. Rest in the promises of God today and know that although your sin is a big deal, your God has an even bigger will!

DAY 015

1. When you sin what does God say about you? How do you know this to be true?

____

____

____

____

____

____

____

____

____

____

2. As a result of your sin are you often left feeling convicted and judged, or convicted to become more righteous? ____

____

____

____

____

____

____

____

____

____

////// **CHALLENGE:** Develop a reverse reaction to sin in your life. The next time you find yourself in sin, don't run from the Father run to Him. Don't pay twice for what was already paid for once through Christ. ____

____

____

____

____

____

____

____

____

____

LORD,

I am often challenged to avoid you when I feel I have failed you and sinned. Please help me to think with a redeemed mind that Christ paid for my sins and afforded me forgiveness. I am no longer condemned when I fall short. Allow me to live in the fullness of what it means to be restored according to your will. In Jesus' Name,

AMEN.

DAY 016

"The gospel only becomes good news when you tell someone, otherwise its just news."

DAY 016

But how can they call on him to save them unless they believe in him? And how can they believe in him if they have never heard about him? And how can they hear about him unless someone tells them?

ROMANS 10:14 (NLT)

The term gospel is one that is often regarded as a doctrine of prime importance or something that is true and implicitly believed. This term is derived from the secular understanding of the word gospel. Ponder on the knowledge that you have of what the gospel means, according to the Bible, as to the creation of all things, the fall of mankind (and that same creation), Jesus Christ coming to redeem all men, and the future restoration of all things. Now imagine the significance of its impact. This is why it is called good news because anyone who hears and understands it will see the beauty of our God and His love for all His creation. This is also why our Lord has stressed so emphatically that we make it our lives business to share it. This gospel message that we preach gives life to its hearers because full restoration of His Kingdom is coming and a glimpse is revealed in you today! Make sure you take the opportunity today to do more than just harvest this news, but share it with someone else. Stop waiting for people to come visit your church or ask you about your faith. By now you should know that the church is not a place but it is both you and I. The power of the living church and the body of believers is revealed as we go, the gospel travels with and through us. The good news of Jesus Christ has the power to transform the life of the one receiving it as soon as it is understood. Don't deprive your neighbors, co-workers, family members, or friends of that privilege today. What if someone didn't share that news with you? Where would you be?

DAY 016

1. When you first heard the good news how was it shared to you and how did you respond? ____

____

____

____

____

____

____

____

____

____

2. If you could go back to the first time you heard the good news what would you change about that experience? Think about it on behalf of not only yourself but the individual sharing it as well. ____

____

____

____

____

____

____

____

____

////// **CHALLENGE:** Take the critiques that you mentioned in question #2 and use them to strengthen how you will share the good news with someone today. Enhance the experience for the next person by giving them a better presentation of the truth than you had. If you love God, keep His commands and share the Gospel of the Kingdom of God.

____

____

____

____

____

____

____

____

DEAR LORD,

soften my heart to be more sensitive to others around me that have never heard your life changing message. I know that I can overlook the responsibility to share the good news but I pray that you would help me to fully understand it that I may share with boldness and confidence to those around me. In Jesus' Name,

AMEN.

DAY 017

//////////////

"Your advocate defends you, when you can't get through the trial."

//////////////

DAY 017

My dear children, I write this to you so that you will not sin. But if anybody does sin, we have an advocate with the Father - Jesus Christ, The Righteous One.

1 JOHN 2:1 (NIV)

An advocate does not excuse your condemnation or your just punishment for breaking the law by rationalizing and reasoning with your actions that opposed the law. Rather, if that advocate is law abiding and is good at what he does, he will plead your case before your accuser with such convincing evidence, that the judge and jury will grant you mercy, even though he knew you should have been found guilty. That is the nature of our King Jesus! It has nothing to do with you and I. We are guilty, but we have an Advocate and He has never lost a case. The dynamic part about this case is that the law is just and rightfully condemns us, but we are under grace! Why do we have grace you may ask? Every time we are to be condemned, Jesus our Advocate shows the Judge the settlement offer (His Blood, thorny brow, scarred back and nail pierced feet and hands). It is a reminder to the Judge that a "not guilty" verdict was rendered and the case against us shall be dismissed. The sacrifice of Christ settled the wrath of God and we received the gift of eternal life in exchange for the punishment of death for our sins. God never accepts sinners, He only accepts Christ. So today look at what you are going through as a trial, and remember you have an Advocate. Put your trust in Him especially when you fall short for he orchestrated the best type of plea bargain in your defense.

DAY 017

1. How does viewing Jesus as an advocate on your behalf pleading your case of innocence change the way you view God's judgment?______________________________

2. What trials/tests have you faced lately that you have failed or fallen victim to?

DAY 017

////// **CHALLENGE:** Strive to live today completely in the Spirit of God and not sin. If you do sin, approach Jesus immediately in prayer and repentance understanding He is your advocate. Watch what a difference it makes! ______________________________

____

____

____

____

____

____

____

____

____

JESUS,

thank you for being an advocate on my behalf and pleading my innocence in the places I was guilty. I thank you for never leaving me. Thank you for becoming not only my advocate but ransoming your life as the plea bargain that has granted my innocence. I am ever grateful to you for seeing me past my guilt. In your name,

AMEN.

DAY 018

“The Father of Lies sometimes tells the truth about you.”

DAY 018

Or do you not know that the unrighteous will not inherit the kingdom of God? Do not be deceived: neither the sexually immoral, nor idolaters, nor adulterers, nor men who practice homosexuality, nor thieves, nor the greedy, nor drunkards, nor revilers, nor swindlers will inherit the kingdom of God. And such were some of you. But you were washed, you were sanctified, you were justified in the name of the Lord Jesus Christ and by the Spirit of our God.

1 CORINTHIANS 6:9-11 (ESV)

Perhaps you've heard it said that you are worthless, a screw up, a disappointment, an embarrassment, a bad spouse, a terrible parent, the black sheep, a sinner, a hypocrite or even worse. The interesting thing about Satan, the Father of Lies, is that he sometimes tells the truth. All these things you once were, however, he forgets to mention the majestic ending to those indictments is that JESUS SAVES! That's right. Jesus picked you up out your mess and made you holy and is still making you holy through sanctification! The Bible teaches us that this is the will of God that you be sanctified (1 Thessalonians 4:3). Don't get caught up in Satan's half-truth that you don't realize it was a whole lie. You are a new creation in Christ Jesus, old things have passed away...behold all things have been made – YOU!

1. Understanding that you are a new creature in Christ, identify what lies Satan has been speaking to you or about you. ____

____

____

____

____

____

____

____

____

____

2. Sometimes the Father of Lies will orchestrate a way to bring you back to the truths of your painful past. When that happens, how do you respond? _______________________

____

____

____

____

____

____

____

____

____

DAY 018

////// **CHALLENGE:** For every lie that you readily identified, find the corresponding truth for it in God's word and commit it to memory. Walk in the knowledge of who you are according to the truth. ____

____

____

____

____

____

____

____

____

____

____

GOD,

I will admit in the past I have believed some of the lies that were whispered to me from the Father of Lies. I reject them all today in exchange for your truth of who you say I am and I choose to live in that alone. In Jesus Name,

AMEN.

DAY 019

“Repentance is not a request, it is a requirement.”

DAY 019

From that time Jesus began to preach, and to say,
Repent: for the kingdom of heaven is at hand.

MATTHEW 4:17 (KJV)

The first step to walking in the newness of life is denying your own will and agenda. It is often very difficult to redirect our motives or change our frame of mind, especially if our plans are firmly established. When it comes to us, things are pretty concrete. After all, we are said to exhibit a heart of stone at times. To this end, repentance, or changing your mind is not a request; rather it is a requirement for holy living and entering the Kingdom of God. The first word spoke of Jesus' public ministry and the cry of John the Baptist, His forerunner, was REPENT! Rather than a worldly, surface level sorrow, repentance stems from a recognition and confession of our depraved state of mind or hearts of stone and actively turning from it. Once we come to grips with the fact that sin is a mind and heart issue and not simply our actions, true healing can begin. Repentance is required for salvation because it helps us to see our sin as God sees it; in our hearts and minds. It also gives us true appreciation for the value of the cross, the beauty and grace found in the gospel, and clear understanding of our mission while here on earth. Today don't look at repentance as a simple suggestion, but see it for what it truly is, a change in light of the truth towards renewed minds and purified hearts.

DAY 019

1. What are some things in your life that you and God don't see eye to eye on? Be honest with yourself. ____

____

____

____

____

____

____

____

____

____

2. If you and God disagree about a particular area in your life, whom do you think most likely is wrong? Why? ____

____

____

____

____

____

____

____

____

____

////// **CHALLENGE:** If you and God have some differences concerning the areas of your life, humble yourself and repent. Take a moment in prayer and openly acknowledge your faults and give them willingly to God that your heart and mind might be changed. _____

____

____

____

____

____

____

____

____

____

____

LORD,

I know that I have areas in my life that are in desperate need of change. Help me to honestly identify them as I approach you in prayer concerning my faults. Help me to continually grow in and through repentance. In Jesus' Name,

AMEN.

DAY 020

“Got influence? Use it wisely… you will be judged for it.”

DAY 020

In everything set them an example by doing what is good. In your teaching show integrity, seriousness and soundness of speech that cannot be condemned, so that those who oppose you may be ashamed because they have nothing bad to say about us.

TITUS 2:7-8 (NIV)

God takes stewardship over His resources and people very seriously. Woe to those who mismanage them! If God has placed you in a position of power or influence whether in the corporate world, your home, ministry, or in the community, it's your responsibility to act with wisdom and prudence. Integrity is the common thread all God's leaders ought to rest upon as He holds them to a higher standard, and His judgment is keener towards those caring for His people. Be careful about always taking the lead if you are not ready to handle the responsibilities, consequences, and rewards that come with it. Many situations we walk into have been damaged prior to us arriving, and are of no fault of our own. Nevertheless, as a kingdom citizen when you choose to walk the narrow road you assume responsibility even for those things that you are faultless for, which are now under your care. Evaluate your position today and make adjustments where necessary to be the best leader in every situation.

1. Name an example when you have witnessed or experienced someone wielding his or her influence in a negative way.

2. Do you believe that you have influence over others? How does your answer affect the decisions you make?

DAY 020

////// **CHALLENGE:** Track one or two individual's lives you influence whether directly or indirectly. Ask them what they think the most consistent attribute is about you. The response may reveal an answer that you were not aware you had an influence in. Take your time to make improvements if necessary. ____________________________________

____

____

____

____

____

____

____

____

____

GOD,

I thank you for the lives I encounter and those whom I have influence over. Thank you for the privilege of being in a position of responsibility. Keep me humble and open with a willingness to change, perfect, and improve for your names sake. In Jesus' Name,

AMEN.

DAY 021
"Being fully restored
is always better
than covering up."

DAY 021

Instead of shame and dishonor, you will enjoy a double share of honor. You will possess a double portion of prosperity in your land, and everlasting joy will be yours.

ISAIAH 61:7 (NLT)

The world has told you to cover up mistakes to make yourself happy. You don't like your hair? Cut it, dye it, or get a wig or weave. If you have a blemish, use cosmetics to mask it away. If you don't like your gender or orientation - change it. If you don't want the baby - abort it. Do you need more money? Withhold information on your taxes, etc. The problem with the "cover up" mentality is that it doesn't result in true lasting happiness, and we divert from our primary purpose by trying to create an alternate route. God is looking to restore you to His original image that He created you in, to continue bringing glory to Himself. It is His delight that you would prosper, be content, and be completely satisfied in Him alone. Come to Christ with your mistakes and broken moments and let Him restore them and make you whole in it and build you through it. True restoration looks better on you than the counterfeit cover up.

1. In what ways do you seek satisfaction or contentment that rests outside of God's provision? ______________________________

2. How has temporarily covering up areas in your life that need to be made whole, affected your relationship with God? ______________________________

////// **CHALLENGE:** Search your heart in this moment to see why you haven't trusted God to bring you complete satisfaction in those areas of your life. Ask Him earnestly to change you. ____

____

____

____

____

____

____

____

____

____

____

DEAR GOD,

I come to you openly and honestly knowing that I haven't been fully satisfied in you alone. Reveal to me what it is that keeps me from fully trusting you and your word. In Jesus' Name,

AMEN.

DAY 022

//////////////

"God will not do a new thing with your circumstances until He first does a new thing in you. Heart change is required first."

//////////////

DAY 022

…one of His disciples said to Him, 'Lord, teach us to pray…'

LUKE 11:1 (KJV)

How many times have you heard the saying "if I just had this or if I just had that, then I would do this"? The human psyche is conditioned to believe that external stimuli controls behavior or permanently alters emotional states of satisfaction. This is the farthest thing from the truth. God understands the genetic makeup of our fallen state and will not do anything new around us until a change inside of us has taken place first. Once the heart of a person is regenerated then their response to the external stimuli will change no matter what it is. God invests in change that occurs in the heart, which is lasting. So today, challenge yourself to stop praying only about your situation and to start praying for a renewed mind and pure heart. One purpose of prayer is that it is designed to change us. Prayer frames our world with God's Word thereby turning us from victims of our circumstances, to becoming more than conquerors. Use your power today!

1. Why do you think we prefer our circumstances to be changed as opposed to our hearts?

2. When you are facing a tough situation that seems out of control how do you typically handle it? Do you blame God or ask Him for help?

DAY 022

////// **CHALLENGE:** The prayer portion of today has been left blank. Take some time and write down the circumstances you are currently facing and then approach God in prayer and petition. Remember not to take the stance of simply asking Him to change it but to change your heart and outlook instead. ______________________________

____

____

____

____

____

____

____

____

____

LORD,

DAY | 023

"If you had the pleasure to open your eyes this morning and you have breath in your lungs, then you have a responsibility to praise God; anything less would be simply disrespectful."

DAY 023

Let everything that has breath praise the LORD. Praise the LORD.

PSALM 150:6 (NIV)

Take a moment to think about this: In His infinite power and wisdom the Creator of the universe has decided to work his omnipotent hands in the realm of time, reached out from eternity to ensure that you woke up this morning. Once again, He has graced you to breathe peacefully while you slept and restored you back to consciousness today. For no other reason than Christ himself being the sustainer of life, He deserves a thank you and acknowledgement as you go throughout your day. To think it was by your own strength, strict diet, sleeping regiment, or control that allowed you to rest and rise again, would be simply distasteful. God owns the very breath circulating in your body as you read this page. Give Him His credit as you come and go, for some are not as fortunate to have the privilege to have done so today.

1. How do you suppose not acknowledging the Lord's role in being the sustainer of life can affect a person's mood, decisions, and relationships? ______________________________

____

____

____

____

____

____

____

____

____

2. NARROW MINDED individuals are naturally different and are presumed as focused on one particular thing. In our case, the difference maker and focal point is Jesus. Write down how your moods, decisions, and relationships differ from the rest of society. _________

____

____

____

____

____

____

____

DAY 023

////// **CHALLENGE:** Praise God for the immeasurable things that He has done for you over the last 22 days with the breath of life that was given to you. ________________

____

____

____

____

____

____

____

____

____

FATHER,

thank you for giving me the gift of life and breath in my body to honor and serve you. Allow me to always be reminded of your goodness and to never let a day go by without expressing my gratefulness. In Jesus' Name,

AMEN.

DAY 024

"If your money controls your attitude, by default it controls your faith."

DAY 024

Keep your life free from love of money, and be content with what you have, for he has said, "I will never leave you nor forsake you."

HEBREWS 13:5 (ESV)

Money can have a very powerful hold over ones mood, men specifically in my experiences. For a man not to have any money there is an inexplicable irritation with life as well as questions that begin to form within him. He starts questioning his worth and purpose as a man and his ability to provide. He questions the faithfulness and sovereignty of God's promises. At times he may even question if he is on this journey alone. Women are known to have some of the same feelings as well. When we have an affectionate love for money we no longer look at it as something God has blessed us with as a means, but we change our outlook to it being MY end and MY own possession. Idolatry is in full effect when money controls your faith and attitude, revealing that your belief in it is greater than your belief in God. Instead of allowing it to remain a resource, you replace it as The Source. While momentary frustrations arise naturally with financial strain, don't allow them to stay there. If you find yourself constantly frustrated and lashing out because things aren't going in your favor with the almighty dollar, analyze who and what you are putting your trust in. Money comes and goes, but God remains in spite of!

DAY 024

1. You've just won $1,000,000. Write down exactly what you would do with the money until it's all spent. Account for every dollar. ______________________________

____

____

____

____

____

____

____

____

____

2. How would you be able to identify if money has a grip on your attitude when you are allocating the money? ______________________________

____

____

____

____

____

____

____

____

____

DAY 024

////// **CHALLENGE:** Examine where the three major amounts of money were allocated in question #1. Ask yourself the question is this where your genuine faith lies? ________

____

____

____

____

____

____

____

____

____

LORD,

reveal to me my need for you alone and help me to trust that you will never leave me. Direct my heart to invest in the Kingdom of God and the things that bring about your good pleasure. In Jesus' Name,

AMEN.

DAY 025

"Your darkness diminishes only with exposure to the Light."

DAY 025

But everything exposed by the light becomes visible –
and everything that is illuminated becomes a light.

EPH. 5:13 (NIV)

In each and every one of us lies a darkness that we try to get rid of. It is the darkness of our sub consciousness, the impure thoughts and hidden motives, the evil things of our past. This darkness, if left alone will attempt to overtake us unless we have exposure to the light source. When the light shows up, darkness excuses itself from the scene. It is exposed and it diminishes in the face of the light. The darkness cannot stand the light. The Bible teaches us "the light shines in the darkness, and the darkness has not overcome it." – John 1:5 (NIV) Jesus is the Word of God and in that He is the light. Regardless of what areas of darkness you are dealing with today, the challenge you have is to expose yourself to the true Light, be seen for who you are, then allow Him to change you. Light will not only change you but it will also expose those areas that you had hidden in the darkness. Before you are cleansed you have to come to grips with your current condition and agree something must change.

DAY 025

1. What have you hidden in darkness in hopes that others wouldn't find it and Christ won't touch it? ____

____

____

____

____

____

____

____

____

____

2. How does not dealing with unresolved issues in your heart and mind affect your prayer life? ____

____

____

____

____

____

____

____

____

____

DAY 025

////// **CHALLENGE:** Stop holding back. Submit the past, the impure thoughts, and the uncovered agendas/motives to God. Open up the chamber where they lie in darkness, that those things too may become illuminated as light!______________________________

____

____

____

____

____

____

____

____

____

LORD,

I'm coming to you opening up the deep dark places within me and giving you full access. Sweep me clean with your truth and Holy Spirit and convict me unto righteousness. Free me from my past, remove the impurities in my thoughts, and redirect my hearts motives. In Jesus' Name,

AMEN.

DAY 026

"If you're not sharing your faith, you may not have a true belief in the eternal hope."

DAY 026

I am not ashamed of the gospel, because it is the power of God
for the salvation of everyone who believes...

ROMANS 1:16 (KJV)

Faith is BELIEF in action. If you believe something enough you will share it uncontrollably because you truly believe in it. What are the things you share the most? Do they line up with your gospel profession? If not, you must re-examine your belief system. There are a lot of people just one demeaning comment away from suicide, one bed away from giving themselves to the first person to show them false love and affection (be it hetero or homo), one bottle away from overdosing on prescription drugs hoping to never wake up again, or one bullet away from playing Russian roulette with their lives. Think about them the next time you profess to intimately know the God of love while remaining a closed mouth Christian. Jesus brought hope to others concerning the Kingdom along with a new way of thinking, not just a religion. Since you bear His name, what are you bringing to them? It's time to start bearing His image and bringing His message!

DAY 026

1. Christ in the physical is seen in you. In what ways can you make this day different and share your faith? ____________________

2. Do most people you interact with on a daily basis know how committed to Christ you are? How do you know? ____________________

DAY 026

////// **CHALLENGE:** Talk to two complete strangers today about your faith and unending hope in Jesus Christ. Challenge yourself to remove the classic model of evangelism and do it in a way that is personal and authentic. ____________________

____

____

____

____

____

____

____

____

____

JESUS,

I know that I love you and I want to not only wear your name as a title but also reflect your image here on earth. Help me to set my mind towards those individuals who are lost and without hope so I can point them to you and the work you've done on the cross. In Your Name,

AMEN.

DAY 027

“Your humility is prideful.”

DAY 027

"The Pharisee stood and was praying this to himself: 'God, I thank You that I am not like other people: swindlers, unjust, adulterers, or even like this tax collector. I fast twice a week; I pay tithes of all that I get.' But the tax collector, standing some distance away, was even unwilling to lift up his eyes to heaven, but was beating his breast, saying, 'God, be merciful to me, the sinner!' I tell you, this man went to his house justified rather than the other; for everyone who exalts himself will be humbled, but he who humbles himself will be exalted."

LUKE 18:11-14 (NASB)

Have you ever met people who shy away from opportunities or voluntarily put themselves down? God requires us not to be haughty in spirit, prideful, or boastful in our own abilities. However, there is a distinct difference between true humility and false modesty. False modesty is cloaked with the thin veneer of a humble individual, while its true intent is to be celebrated for taking a position of lesser value. The one who seeks notoriety for their humility, is really much more prideful and deceptive than the one who petitions outward approval for their accomplishments. Be careful not to fall into this trap of receiving praise for exhibiting a false spirit of humility. God has been calling you to some great things. Yet, you have been proudly declining because of your fear or your desire to choose the "politically correct" Christian response of humility. Listen to the Holy Spirit today and remove your pride.

1. Have you ever dealt with false modesty/humility? Did you overcome it?

If so how?____

2. Why do you think false humility is so dangerous in the life of a believer? __________

////// **CHALLENGE:** See it the way God sees it. False humility is rooted in deception, which is the tool of Satan, the Father of lies. If you pinpoint any of it in your life, extract it immediately so that you may be seen as a child of the Light. ______________________

____

____

____

____

____

____

____

____

____

GOD,

first please forgive me for being false in my modesty and humility. I don't want to misrepresent you and I don't want to convey a prideful attitude by turning down opportunities. Allow me to remain authentic in every way. Let my Yes be Yes and my No be No. In Jesus Name,

AMEN.

"A life that is focused on you and what you are doing all the time for/through/in the name of God is not the same as a life focused on God and what He is doing in you."

DAY 028

Therefore, my beloved, as you have always obeyed, so now, not only as in my presence but much more in my absence, work out your own salvation with fear and trembling, for it is God who works in you, both to will and to work for his good pleasure.

PHIL. 2:12-13 (ESV)

As you journey through your walk with Christ, once you've learned the basic principles of the Christian faith, life tends to become hectic. For some, a fraction of the initial passion is replaced with religious routine. The misconception sweeping across our nation is that we must complete a work or do things in His name to maintain our Christendom. To make it plain, many Christians still believe they must merely "do" good works alone to keep up with their Christian title. Jesus plainly stated in Matthew 7:22, that many would do works in His name and still would not inherit eternal life. God is not simply seeking servants who work robotically to appease the expectations of men or meet the requirements of religion. God is looking for us to serve Him and to intimately know Him so that our obedience may produce good works as a result of our relationship with Him. In order to be a worthy disciple of the Lord Jesus Christ, we must spend time getting to know Him. How can one come to know God you may ask? Avoid getting busy in His name simply because you have His title. But rather throw yourself recklessly in the abundance of His holy attributes. Seek, through the understanding provided by the Holy Spirit, exactly who the God you serve is, and what He has purposed for your life. By doing so, you will save a lot of time and performance of insincere service. Perhaps He doesn't reveal all the answers to you right away, but the peace of knowing that He has a plan and that you are pursuant to discovering it is far better than blindly attempting to serve Him without understanding His will.

DAY 028

1. What are some ways you could "throw yourself recklessly in the abundance of God's Holy attributes" without just doing the work of the Lord? ____________________

____

____

____

____

____

____

____

____

____

2. What aspect of God are you uncertain about that you'd like to learn more of and perhaps is not taught often enough in your church? ____________________

____

____

____

____

____

____

____

____

____

DAY 028

////// **CHALLENGE:** Substitute one of the minor routine activities that you do for the Lord, and spend time getting to know more about the attribute or area you mentioned by studying His word. Then, if you desire, ask Him to reveal Himself to you in that way so you can truly experience Him intimately based off your study. ______________________________

____

____

____

____

____

____

____

____

____

FATHER,

I don't just want to know about you and work for you, but I long to know you personally and experience you intimately. Help me to refocus my affections on you in Jesus Name,

AMEN.

DAY 029

"If you're in a storm, instead of looking for relief, take refuge – you may be here for a while."

DAY 029

God is our refuge and strength, a very present help in trouble.

PSALM 46:1 (KJV)

Let's face it; life is full of what we call "trials" or "storms". An old common phrase is if you are not in a storm currently you are either coming out of one or going into another. The point is that trials are ever-present and so you must learn how to survive through it. You may be facing a series of trials relationally, financially, or spiritually that you are crying out for God to relieve you from. You wish He would make them all go away or perhaps He would swoop down and save you from them. If you (like many others) have gone to God in prayer and afterward realized that the storm not only persisted but also has gotten even worse, you may start to feel discouraged. Don't give up! Here is the hope that in our trials/storms God is not instructing us to seek relief or complain that the situation changes. The way you will get through it is by taking refuge in Him alone. To take refuge means you have found a safe place to camp out for a while until whatever is going on passes you by. Here is the beauty about taking refuge in God, while there He will give you strength to endure. As sure as the storm is present God is also a very present help in the time of trouble. So today, if you feel like you barely have the strength to make it through the storm and you're tired of asking God to make it stop, you are in a good place. Stop crying and run to Him for refuge. Ask Him to strengthen you by the Holy Spirit and see how differently the storm will look. Give it some time and soon you'll be dancing in the rain.

1. Name a situation or a trial that you would rather God take you out of, than be your refuge in. ____

____

____

____

____

____

____

____

____

____

2. What benefits would you gain by God stopping the trial you mentioned above or Him removing you from it?____

____

____

____

____

____

____

____

____

____

////// **CHALLENGE:** Think critically, how does God get glory out of your answers above? If He doesn't, change your heart and renew your mind to see how His refuge in the trial is a better relief than a rescue from it. ______________________________

____

____

____

____

____

____

____

____

____

DEAR GOD,

open the eyes of my heart so I can see you in all the trials of my life. Allow me to see your hand at work in the areas where you are trying to strengthen me. Help me to realize I am blessed when I go through things because you are with me. If there is anything inside of me that is keeping me from trusting you completely, remove it. In Jesus' Name,

AMEN.

DAY 030

//////////////

"God realizes you came to fly with baggage but He says, "check that stuff at the gate, I got it." You're allowed one carry on – let's make it a cross!"

//////////////

DAY 030

Then He said to them all: "Whoever wants to be my disciple must deny themselves and take up their cross daily and follow me.

LUKE 9:23 (NIV)

Coming to terms with knowing that how you've been living is not cutting it, begs one question; where else can I go? If you have trusted the Lord Jesus Christ you've decided to fly high and take a ride with Him simply by grace alone through faith alone. The problem is you brought your baggage...but after all isn't that what He tells us to do? Only difference with this trip is, He didn't tell you to bring your baggage along for the journey, He wants you to check it at the gate for an exchange. Wait a minute; you loved that baggage though. You kept it hidden away in your closet, it has your name stitched on it, you safeguard it with your life when you travel, and you made sure it contains all you will ever need. One could assume that when you are away from home, in a foreign place your entire identity is stored in your baggage. However, here's the offer you get when you come to the gate – drop your baggage here and in exchange you are allowed one carry on; a cross. You will learn to love this cross. As much as you think your baggage helped you, it only held you down, but this cross is going to help you get through the turbulence. Put down the baggage of your life today and take on the cross of Christ in His righteousness. Watch how your burdens become lighter as you enjoy your elevation in trusting Him alone.

DAY 030

1. What in your life is keeping you from soaring with Christ that you just can't seem to let go of? ____________________

____

____

____

____

____

____

____

____

____

2. Why do you feel as if you cannot substitute those baggage items with the loving Savior who satisfies your every need? ____________________

____

____

____

____

____

____

____

____

____

////// **CHALLENGE:** Fly with one carry on – The Cross. This is called a faith flight. For one day set all your habits and dependent safety nets aside. Trust God in every decision you make throughout your day. ______________________________

____

____

____

____

____

____

____

____

____

GOD,

I am coming to you with my hands clenched tightly around some things that I have put my whole hope in. Please help me to release them and to trust you completely. I check my baggage in the form of idols, source of dependency, past sin that are keeping me bound, and those things that seek to identify me. I cling to your cross. In Jesus' Name,

AMEN.

DAY 031

"If you have to constantly remember to ACT like a Christian, it's time to check the character in the scene."

DAY 031

. . . for you have stripped off your old sinful nature and all its wicked deeds. Put on your new nature, and be renewed as you learn to know your Creator and become like him.

COLOSSIANS 3:9B-10 (NLT)

After the resurrection of Jesus Christ and the dispensing of the Holy Spirit, the early Apostles became one hundred percent committed to the cause of Christ. The question we often ask; 'how is your spiritual life', to them would be the same as 'how are you doing'? For them those two questions were one in the same. Though they had their faults, their identity was found in Christ alone. There was no mutually exclusive spiritual life versus a normal life. What about you? Do you go through your days, living as a person of true integrity and character, committed to the cause of Christ? Or perhaps you just play a character called The Christian, sprinkling the scene with shallow temporary piety before going off-set to be the real you again. True Christians are followers of The Way who need not act or attempt to modify their behavior to love Christ, His Word, other people, or His Church any more than a recently newborn baby needs to act hungry or a child needs to act like they love their parents. They just do. The key is immersing yourself in Christ and allowing the Holy Spirit to be operable in you so that He would continually change your heart and allow your actions to follow. Actions replace actors and true character will replace characters.

DAY 031

1. What kinds of "scenes" or "settings" have caused you to act differently and depict a character other than that of a true disciple? ____________________

2. Why do these settings, scenes, or situations have so much power over how you project yourself to others? ____________________

////// **CHALLENGE:** Destroy the idols that make you submit to their expectations and compromise the true character of Christ within you. Examine who/what those idols are in each of those settings and seek repentance so you may be one hundred percent authentic in any setting. ____

DEAR LORD,

I only seek to represent you well and to make your name great. Forgive me if I have been acting differently within certain settings. I want to emulate you in every way, every day of my life. Help me to place nothing before you. If I have built up those idols, I submit them to your authority to be destroyed, so that you would receive the glory from my life.

In Jesus' Name,

AMEN.

About the Author

Preacher | Teacher | Author | Ministry-Strategist

Dante Moore is a passionate believer and advocate for the Kingdom of God. As a change agent in the city of Philadelphia, he enjoys laboring among the people of God to make sustainable impact and build leaders through the gospel. His mission is to co-labor among believers to help extract their full potential, by way of exposing their identity in Christ that they may properly live out the gospel in their context.

Over the years Dante has had the opportunity to serve local communities, speak at college campuses, urban outreach events, conferences, workshops, panels, and much more. In addition to the release of his first book, he along with his wife D'ani Moore are spear-heading Made 4 Moore, as they work together to help unveil to the world how success is measured in a life of purpose lived out. In addition, the Moore's continue to cultivate the vision of the citywide non-profit ministry Project (215), Inc. started in 2008 to re-implement it throughout the city of Philadelphia.

Stay tuned for more published works and upcoming releases at:
www.Made4Moore.com

Get in touch with Dante!

@iamdantemoore

@iamdantemoore

@iamdantemoore

@iamdantemoore

Notes

Made in the USA
Middletown, DE
06 October 2018